Soul
Reflections

Soul
Reflections

OF A ROADSIDE PHILOSOPHER

SILOGAN PILLAY

BALBOA.
PRESS

A DIVISION OF HAY HOUSE

Balboa Press books may be ordered through booksellers or by contacting:

Balboa Press
A Division of Hay House
1663 Liberty Drive
Bloomington, IN 47403
www.balboapress.com
1-(877) 407-4847

Because of the dynamic nature of the Internet, any web addresses or
links contained in this book may have changed since publication and
may no longer be valid. The views expressed in this work are solely those
of the author and do not necessarily reflect the views of the publisher,
and the publisher hereby disclaims any responsibility for them.

The author of this book does not dispense medical advice or prescribe the use
of any technique as a form of treatment for physical, emotional, or medical
problems without the advice of a physician, either directly or indirectly. The
intent of the author is only to offer information of a general nature to help
you in your quest for emotional and spiritual well-being. In the event you use
any of the information in this book for yourself, which is your constitutional
right, the author and the publisher assume no responsibility for your actions.

Any people depicted in stock imagery provided by Thinkstock are models,
and such images are being used for illustrative purposes only.
Certain stock imagery © Thinkstock.

ISBN: 978-1-4525-3252-3 (sc)
ISBN: 978-1-4525-3254-7 (e)

Library of Congress Control Number: 2011901624

Printed in the United States of America

Balboa Press rev. date: 3/3/2011

My special thanks goes to Shadika, my loving daughter for corresponding with Balboa Press and editing and typing my work. She's been an indispensible part of this project. I am fully indebted to her for her input. I also acknowledge the support of my wife who has shown determination and fortitude in the trying times of our life.

Part 1

PASSING THOUGHTS

INTRODUCTION

There is much to be given
Of the little you have
Give it now
For tomorrow
Who knows
If it's yours
As promised

MOTHER NATURE

The caterpillar never knew its beauty
until it became a butterfly
The spider is never taught to spin a web
There is no school to teach it
The bat does well without sight
And the tadpole never knew it would be a frog one day
Shed the form and think of the wonder of it all
Of you and me
Where is this hidden knowledge?
Is it in the questioning when you rebel and take charge?
Is that where it's at?
Is that the point where nature reveals its wonder?
Move through Her Hands and be moulded by her thought
Keep a vigilant eye to what She shows you
The purpose of life is not what you and I are made to see
That is just a part of the fabric of life
Meant to deter you and I from the one true light
It is what we are forced to see and do that keeps
This unsteady structure in place
It is not a solid foundation
But a force keeping our thoughts
In alignment for control and predictability
The textbooks we study are a means to a desired end
Knowledge is greater than we make it out to be
Life accommodates all
The seeker will see the farce as clear as daylight
The wise one's are silent for they know
It is not there but here
Feel it, know it, breathe it and be it
That is all there is
And all that is that

M E

Thoughts flow in and out
Like delightful electrons dancing
In the light and then disappearing
In a flash I have condensed
Time and space into a brief memory
As I journey from nowhere to now here.
Out of nothingness I came spinning
Through dimensions unknown and unquestioned,
Gravitating to what I now am.
What a magical play of images
Flash in my memory of you
And I and everything that is
I dematerialized the material
And clung onto the substance of the true metal of my being
- so illusive yet so miraculous,
A wondrous play of sounds and sights
That make up me

MOTHER

Under the cover of
Peaceful understanding of what is
I stand alone
On a deserted beach
Waves of tears
Roll down my cheeks
Images of your presence
Your grace and love
Weighs heavy on my chest
This separation is hard
To bear
Yet I am grateful
For you blessing my life
Words can say so much
Feelings can move you to tears
Knowing you is like being
Part of you
So much give and take
But now just Emptiness,
Blankness, Darkness
Interjected by fleeting moments
Of light
Amidst the memories I bear of you

MOTHER AFRICA

Mother Africa your child longs to be in your arms
You have taught me the tolerance I bear
Of racial discrimination and cultural differences
I carry with me the pride I have
To have been born on South African soil
Where the two great oceans meet
And the San left paintings for all to see
Of Springbok roaming free
I have in me the tongue and tastes
Of an expansive continent
Africa
That bore the seeds of early civilization
You taught me well
To know hunger and pain amidst opulence and greed
And yet to be myself
My spirit bears the stamp resilience
And lies firmly anchored to its moorings
Mother Africa I salute you
I am your child

WIFE

Like a breadth of fresh air
She breezed into my life
Agreeing on unconditional support
We gave our all unquestioned in trust
Forming a sacred bond
Life has it's lessons to teach
And approach to them is to be downright practical
It is our will to see our lives lived
As faith would have it played out
Two souls sealed and stamped by destiny
With a common goal to live life
In peace and harmony
Minus the strife

TO MY DAUGHTER

Your lovingness and sensitivity
Permeates the fabric of our lives,
For it's from the same cloth
That all the qualities we carry are reflected
Whatever lies within is mirrored without
In that same frequency.
It is nature's way of reminding us
Of our presence in the puzzle,
To uphold the balance needed.
We are one,
Living in a matrix of connectivity,
To give off ourselves unselfishly,
And have the pleasure to receive,
The gifts of life
That come unasked.
In this wholesome give and take
May you be blessed for evermore
With inner calm and balance
So that you may find peace
And joy that is your birthright.

494 LOOP STREET

Travelling through present time
Passing places and people of significance
Come in and out
Touching upon memories of an era
Gone by
Every step in human relations is never
To be replayed at the same pitch
As some live with constant regret
While others are overly anxious of the future
Precious time is wasted
The stark reality is that
The "now" is to be lived
As a gift to spread love and peace
Visions of yesteryear fill my mind
As I walk the familiar streets
And hear the sounds I'd heard before
Of local accents and slang
The world is a colourful place
When that cord of attachment to
The land of your birth is reignited
Life becomes pitched at a higher level
Of knowingness of your greater self.
Living life without a spiritual want
Is similar to an anchorless ship
With an unconscious captain.
The depth of life can be measured
By the level at which it is lived
But good memories stay
And old soldiers never die
They just fade away
Like memories of little significance

HOPE

I lay claim to a flame of hope
Deep in my soul that drives me
To places I never meant to travel
And do things I thought I'm never capable of
Just when I lose sight of its golden mane
It makes its appearance felt,
To constantly remind me
It is as perennial as the grass
When I am fired up
I lift the vibrations to a level that brings a smile
Saying all is well.
That's when I dust myself off
Pick up my tools
And feel restored
By a mightier Hand

PATIENCE

The ebb and flow of fluctuating emotions,
On a sea of unpredictable occurrences,
Only brought about by thinking,
In predictable patterns
Of no end solutions-
I ferry my course
With a steadfast mind
Reminding myself constantly
Of the lifetime values I bear
And to the duty of the lives I have yet to live.
This turbulence is of my making
And it can be stemmed if I deem it so.
My bearings are fixed
My choices made
Onward I journey
With honest intentions
Knowing I have a golden opportunity now
To learn what's being taught
By a patient Teacher.

BLISS

With broken tools and a bent back
I set about restoring my dignity.
In men's eyes it appeared
an impossible task
Yet I knew you knew
I could do it.
Night and day I pushed and pulled at
the holy vessel hoping to see and
feel the clarity I now possess
Levitating to peaceful grounds
Transcending common emotions
of getting and spending
I lay claim to the peace that
is mine
This space I guard with pride
Love throbs in my breast
and in this moment of oneness
I feel wanted
I often escape to my tranquility
base only to return with
renewed confidence to address my
role in this cosmic dance

THE JOURNEY

In wondrous delight I walk and play
In this marvellous moment of time and space
Construed to contain my being.
I loved the thrill of the journey
Which takes me to no special place.
It's like going nowhere yet somewhere.
What I consider a lifetime
Is just a brief second spent in cosmic presence,
Yet to you and me it is an eternity.

THE CANDLE

Growing old
The wick gets shorter
The wax has served its purpose
The flame may still burn
But to the observer
That's an indication for another candle.
Everything is dispensable
And replaceable
The only mark that's made
Is the purpose it served.
Is your life worthwhile?
Is it appreciated?
Are you too busy to notice?
The Hand that lit it
Knows its fate
And its purpose.
The candle burns on heedlessly
As for life
It is carried from one day to the next
Within the confines of restrictive thought

THE BEAT

Walk with me
As we travel
In the light of pure being
Shining bright
Making it evident
That the chosen path
Is truly one of enlightenment
No sorrows, or pain
Just the buoyancy of the moment
Kept in motion
By the emotional knowledge
Of constant support
Unrelenting in a sea of turbulence
Stay not aloof
But come close together
And feel the warmth of a heart
Pounding beat for beat
To the call of destiny

WHEN

When you live,
A Life of anxiety for the future
You are burnt out by stress.
When you live,
A life of regret
You forget the "present"
Which is such a precious gift.
When you live,
A life in the moment
Light emanates from your being.
When you live,
A life where material objects
Are an obsession
You drift further and further
Away from the human race.
When you live,
A life where in order to get
You learn to give from the heart,
Yours is the Earth
And everything in it.
When you live,
A life where no sacrifice is too big
You reside in the heart of God.
When you live,
A life traveling the middle road
You understand the fine balance
Required to make some sense of life.
When you live,
A life unchained of social conditioning's
You experience being a child again.
When you live,
A selfish life

You have nothing to give
And nothing to get.
When you live,
A life with myopic vision
You miss the bigger picture
And what's intended for you.
When you live,
A self-centered life
You become cold and clammy.
When you live,
A clannish life
Your thinking is confined to
A tiny box.
When you live,
A life injected with positivity
You have so much to gain.
When you live,
A life in the flow of unconditional universal love
The doors of heaven
Are accessed at will,
And you hold the keys.

THE NOW

Stray not away
From what keeps
The light of your soul alight.
Yours is a predetermined course
Of ethereal groundings.
Being moored to this earth
Sets in motion
Incidences and occurrences
Which were given to you as a lesson
Your pickings will be plenty
If you realize
How impermanent life is
And how vulnerable we are
To the trivial trappings
This world can give us,
And that relationships were meant to be
Just the way they are
Then you will realize
The peace that comes
When inner wants are minimized
And the now which is given as a gift
Is maximized

UNQUESTIONED

In reality we exist
Within a cocoon of make believe
A mindset of collective ideas,
Typified by well worn cultural norms,
Set in motion by those before us,
Unquestioned,
Fashion by time.
No reasonable doubt interferes,
Lest the code be broken,
And that which divides this from that,
And what is, is undisturbed.
It cannot be otherwise.
Existence will be in vain.

The attire we adorn when we are born
Defines our destiny
And ultimately the way the dice will roll
The discrimination
The hasty deductions
The judgments
Made by the haves against the have not's
Is something played out
With the observers role present

But when we descended upon this holy floating vessel
We came to adorn our naked self's with lessons of wisdom
The necessities are provided selfishly
By mother earth which are often taken for granted.
Our conditioned mind begins to construct walls
As we grow
Separating brother from brother and sister from sister.
Our world has become harsher and colder
Our emotions insensitive
We are consumed with xenophobic madness.
Speaking in different tongues,
Living in different households,
And groomed in different faiths,
Yet at the core of our beings we are but human
And what defines ourselves is our human nature
In truth we are all striving for a common
goal which is contentment.

For when the final curtain is drawn
This drama will end
Can you honestly say
You lived your life
Following a path
You believed was
True to you

THE COSMIC CHIME

Bouncing balls of light we are in flight
Across the galaxies hear our plight
We come to play and rest
Upon this heaven of hazy blue
Destroy further not of what is left
Nothing else will materialize
Mother Nature is groaning with the strain
Parallel universes exists within string theories
Hidden in inaccessible states
Our present energies are too distracted
In barbaric pursuits and dead end games
It's focused on global ideological differences
The age old agenda of who's to be on top
Our greater need for survival it seems
Is missing from the script

THE MATRIX

Generalized summations
Of drifting ideologies
Made in passing-
Endorsed
With a personal flair
Of some novel insight
I hear.
Exceptions to reductionist teachings
Never brought to wholeness
In this stale material matrix.
Games with labels and endless statistics
Delights what is said.
That which you and I ignore
Is what is lacking most-
Golden moments usurped by wanton financial strivings
Making unnatural demands
On our better selves.
As you and I willingly sacrifice
The golden qualities
Of the human heart.
The theories we compound are made to rest
With a helpless sigh or with expectant hope
Reflecting the pitiful plight
Of powerful souls
In desperate flight.
Going neither here nor there.

THE MIRROR

Do not wonder why things have
to be this way
They simply are
Accept this magic design and be
merry in your wonderings.
There will be no time for past regrets
and future woes
Time spent in the now
is all that matters.
You were sent to marvel at the
surroundings, that which is you
is beyond that which you see.
Your perception confines
yourself to slavery.
When you see, you see half a truth,
there is a much bigger picture
if you let your insight carry you there,
When you truly see
Then the true light will shine
on you forever
You will attain your balance
with all that is expected of you
Your role will become defined.

MESSAGE FROM A BOX

In rapid haste of see and grab
We fruitlessly strive
For material gain
Denying any spiritual need
To nourish the soul
It's burning us dry of any hope
For a happy balance.
The system is cracking at its seams
Constrictive thought forms are spilling over
Stifling human potential
In a vain effort to gain manageable control
Of simmering madness
Contained in neatly compartmentalized boxes
Nature chaotically contained in little boxes.
But amidst this holy turmoil ancient wisdom revisits.
Having stood the test of time
Flexible, resilient with renewed confidence advances forth
Into a world sceptically attempting to decipher it's uncertainty
What was an "untruth" yesterday is what is true today.
The illusionary paradigm of Maya
Welcomes the weary traveler
And reminding the forgetful audience
Of the Hand that holds the cup.

NATURES MYSTERY

Life's mysteries sped past
As I gazed into her eyes
It spoke of many lives
Some glorious, many tragic
But the passion of life
And the need to fulfil its ends continues
In that cycle
Which baffles the mind
Like a spider spinning a web
The pattern unwinds
Unknown to the weaver
As if destiny calls the tune
The plot, the players, the props
All set according to the directors discretion
A soul bore a noble continence
Fine tuned through love and sorrow
She lay in her bed wide eyed and listless
She was just seven
HIV had the upper hand
And life walked away without a fight
We helplessly watched with nothing to offer
Life is entwined in karmic bonds
As we meander down the passage of time
To finally unshackle our souls of human bondage

DISCORDANCE

Listen to the beat of the drummer within
And respond to the rhythm that brings the natural flow
To mind, body and spirit
You are driven by this beat
Yet very often you pay no attention to it
Thinking that the sound you hear around you
Is much sweeter by far
Then somewhere down the line
You realize how important your very own sound was
If it was not dampened by distracted
echoes of intrusive thoughts
When you took this mantle
You were armed with music of your own
So precious it is
That if not guarded it can be drowned
By those that wish to take control
To gain their own security and profit
Mass accumulation of neglected frequency
Make up the critical balance of popular opinion
Which dictates the way we live our lives
More often distant from what vibrates within you and me

Part 2

THE ANTHOLOGY
OF THE PIED PIPER

THE ANTHOLOGY
OF THE PAID PIPER

I still hear the piper play his music,
Forcing humanity to respond to his subliminal hypnotic call
For total submission.
I was prey to the call once,
And could not live life stripped of the intoxicating
'Me-too' rhythmic tune creating carbon
copies of myself to chime in unison.
Then some magic moment of insight shone through
So effortlessly.
I saw the force behind the piper,
And in that instant
The music shook me loose from its magnetic moorings.
Instead a soothing call I heard
With abundant peace and quiet
Like some soothing balm for a tired spirit.
I stopped questioning the piper,
And as for the people that pay the piper,
I knew they have no eyes to see,
Ears to hear
Or hearts to feel-
Reminisce of beings of yesteryear
Making a mockery of human existence.

I grew impatient and wanted to know more about the piper,
as precious time slipped away (only energy is eternal)
And I groped around in darkness for years
to be exact about fifty,
This music of the media
Enfolded and entrapped me again
In that hypnotic state.
As I followed each note of the piper
The question again arose.
'But pray-who pays the piper and why?'

Night and day
Year in and year out
Dismal, darkness follows
One event into another,
With no hint of enlightening news,
Just the subliminal messages of subjugation
And oppression was all I heard.
With fear in place,
Security a need
And survival a want-
No more was needed to direct the course of human destiny
Which distinctly lay in the hands that paid the piper.

This magic show you and I
Created forced by the enticing music of the piper
Is the illusion of careful nurturing by the director of the show.
How ingenious and yet so simple.
The mind only acknowledges what the
eyes are commanded to see
The ears are made to hear,
The tongue is meant to taste,
And the heart is made to feel.
Total attention to the tune
Is what it takes
To make the system work.
For without this predictable pattern of thought
The system has no control
And those unfortunate ones
That fail to respond to the robotic call
Are left to graze in fields of pain
And solitude
And doubt
And shunned from public places.
We know the greater the compliance the bigger the profit
The phantom who pays the piper
Will have it no other way.

In haste we made to see
This and that on the media screen
Aligned to malign our thoughts and feelings
In any desired direction
We are programmed not to think
This is a privilege of the few
That sit at the top of the pyramid.
Subliminal tones of hidden messages
Groans through our daily life
The tones of what's expected
And what's needed
And whatever your heart is made to desire plays on ceaselessly
Step out of line
And never again will the music enchant,
instead a different tune is heard,
Unknown
To the masters of the show-
The men who pay the piper

In the name of science we decree
The findings we make in glee.
But this is filtered and censored
And selected to surface
Only and only if
It serves some profitable purpose
'That which is not fit for human consumption
Is dangerous to the system', they say
don't be fooled they bear no heed to human need.
The monster that feeds off us
Grows larger and satiated
The pot of gold must glitter
Who cares if man destroys this and that,
'That's his problem-
I must have my pound of flesh

I get bored when you speak of fair play and greater balance.
This sport has no blood in it.
Not for me, I declare.
Let the fools be merry
With their toys of mass distraction
Give them more of those electronic devices
That will surely confuse their DNA.
Keep them busy-the busier they are the less
time there is for them to think or feel.
In this chosen illusion I will take the lot
The day I have your senses
Tied up in knots '
So goes the tune the piper plays.

Philosophers and doctors talk
Wisely of this and that
Schooled into thinking of
What's good for you and me
Their free speech and thought
Aborted by the dictates of decorum
What appears good
And smells of humanity
Does not fit into their scheme of things
The piper knows that tune well.
If he cannot play the required note
we will readily find another
Lured by gold and silver
The piper is dispensable
The music is not-
Play on it must
You cannot break the rhythm
Empires crumble to dust if it stops
But who cares it's only the enchanted
music of power and control.
Play it any way you wish but play on-
It's the opiate that controls the masses
If blood should spill-who cares
If babies die in Africa-who cares
It's the music that has to be played,
so say the people on top, controlling the show.
If the dreaded pill of fear they make us swallow
is no more who can tell what would be the in the reality frame.
Don't stop and step outside
The fresh air you breathe
Is a delusion of satanic peril
And speaks ill of the poor piper
Who will surely burn in hell.

In lonely apartments
People stay warm and sheltered,
With stomachs full from the last meal
In some franchised establishment
Of get-fat food.
In the wide open spaces of intense midnight heat,
Semi-naked people sprawl out to pass the night
Without a morsel of food for days.
Somewhere in the world
in cars and buildings
bombs detonate on a predetermined date
as decided by the powers that be
to create deliberate chaos.
Killing innocent bystanders
Making no selection in whom it chooses.
Amidst all this I distinctly hear
The tune-the piper is paid to play.

He held his clasped hands up above his head.
In humble submission
His punishment
for refusing to hear the music
was prison for twenty seven years in a tiny cell.
But the music he was born with grew
stronger and louder and spread from cell to cell
bursting forth to the world in all its glory.
In his lifetime Mandela did what very few men did,
He created his own music.
The Dalai Lama left his country at the age of seventeen
for no fault of his own and took refuge
in the warmth of the country that
offered their hospitality gladly.
Never has he been back to his land
for his ear refuses to hear the music of despair.
But the piper's play goes only to the highest bidder.
Sadly the Lama's offer is paltry.
The piper cares not for human piety,
It's not his highest scale of payment.
Is this the play we meant to see
or have we been kept in the dark
about the complete agenda
the select few have a much more sinister plot yet to unfold

In one quick sweep we knew
The intention made its mark.
But that very intention was set in motion a long time ago.
It was a result of a tailored result
That's all that's needed to start a war of personal profit
A blatant insult on human intelligence
and total disregard for human suffering.
To kill and maim is inhuman
but to let others take the blame is the order of the day.
The only picture you and I will see is
what the piper currently plays.

The show must go on
The dispensable human resource is insured never to be empty.
Supplies we have plenty.
It's like Harvest - the climax of ultimate pleasure.
The more you get them to sow
The more they will have to show- this is good for business.
In deceptive silence we pride ourselves
With knowledge of some academic nature
But it is the successful makings
Of soulless beings
made to keep systems in place
that benefit just a few-
the few pulling the strings that make the puppets play.
Dominating the realm of pure illusion
People spend their lives
Trying to give definition to their lives
Only to find much later
they took the rap for being a cog in a heartless machine
To be harvested when the need arose.
The piper is made to play
This famous harvest tune only when the moments right.

I have heard you speak
Of changing ideologies for the good of mankind.
I have seen them dismantled in disgust.
The plan has just moved to phase 'B 'of tighter control in fact.
I have seen you ignore the cries of human suffering.
The system is not geared for you and I
to lend a hand without a string attached.
I have seen despots display power
Deplete of any emotions related to the human species
I have seen the lavish extravagance of wealth
amidst abject poverty which secures and approves
'Big Brother's presence.
How else can safety prevail?
I have seen the arrogance of the have's
in the presence of the have-nots
as if they absent of any human feelings.
I am intrigued by the dimension of want and need
where fair play is non-existent.
How repetitive life can be.
A cracked record played to ears
whose minds are programmed not to remember
The giving and receiving of simple human needs
that has no place in the music that comes from the piper.

Sinister Agendas in secret places are held
I am told
covertly designed to set in motion
a plan for total human bondage.
They pay for the cost of the carnage.
Lift the veil that blinds you
And unlock the mind
for in that lies the light to undo the spiritual power
that knows no bindings.
You cannot be trapped in the illusion forever,
it's batteries are running low.
Your allegiance is to the realm of infinite possibilities
The realm of consciousness that is inherently yours and mine.
This truth cannot be bought or sold.
The day you became a reality of pure love (life)
Was the day you entered this energy field which is eternal.
To squander this gift on trivial pursuit-
a purposeless illusion of existence
where you made to play a pawn
is a part of the play we can well do without.
The day we were born
we were whole and defined
We continue to be that way.
Feel the wholeness of 'I'.
In this openness no music will touch you except that of love
It knows no confining box of bones or flesh
It does not conform to the music the piper plays.

I have my own music
It came from the journey I took
Of doubt, ridicule and untold humiliation.
You will walk that path as I did.
You will see the piper
You will hear his music
You will wonder then
why he plays this tune in such a predictable fashion.
You will see power manipulated to makes it so.
Then you will realize the need for release
from the blooded bondage we are trapped within.
For ours is the domain of eternal love
for us to use to set us free
Which opens our world to infinite possibilities.
the only truth you need to know.

Man and women they say
Came to be
Around and apple tree
While the ever present snake took part in the holy deal
The polarity of that moment created a lightning flash
Of guilt and hate and caused,
A movement of desperate souls
yearning to make amends for deeds committed in 'sin'.
How alien this is to the spirit that resides in you and me
For it touches a frustrating note-
The human spirit cannot be clothed in fancy robes
Of any color ,creed or culture
To hide its native nature.
For it will not carry the weight of vain deception
Which is the only unifying power we possess.
If it fails the piper then has his way
And all is lost for a pocket full of promises.

We are packages of energy,
dynamically effected by emotions
reflected off whatever we see and do.
What an experience it is
to feel the intensity of the emotional field.
Emotions are the keys with which
we play our music.
You can take it to any scale you want.
But never is the light so bright
as when the note of love is played
for it's energy sets us free.
Fear sucks our energy away
and never has enough
until we stop and turn the other way
refusing to play and change the energy flow to love...
it is our natural suit of armour.
By repressing fear and expressing love
we steady the holy vessel in a state of wholeness,
Each mortal being listening to the music from their own heart
Free of interfering debris to follow a dance
To the music of love displayed as brilliant energy.
For it is fear that keeps the music playing
to control you and me
so that we do not see who really pays the piper.
They plot and plan schemes
within their ranks
selecting one for this head of state and one for that
while you and I are fooled to believe
we had a vital part to play in this and that
because we trusted and believed
what was said by those that be.

The stakes are so high
that there is no room for chance,
the story of a few hundred people
controlling six billion or more
like they always done.
But the veil is wearing thin,
the energy shield weakens
(fossil fuel cannot do the trick to seal the leak)
So you and I are getting to see,
The created illusion of control
And awake to the presence
of life minus the manipulation.
The ultimate truth,
Beaming through the 'I' that is in you and me.
For it is love setting us finally free.

Part 3

MEMOIRS ON A
NEW YORK SUBWAY

PRESENCE

In restless dreams, and sleepless nights
I search my wakeful hours,
To find that which makes sense
Of this confused state of existence.
That which is- transcends all borders.
It stands out at a given moment
To be defined as it appears
A moment enjoyed in a timeless void
With no constraints of space
Reflecting the beauty of human presence.

MY EXPERIENCE

I traveled the road less traveled
Only to find how much I had learned
The highs were higher
And the lows were deeper
But so was my expansive self
Which grew more resilient with experience

MOVEMENT

Dance to the rhythm
That moves your soul
As you unravel the mystery
Of the marvel that is you

THE PUZZLE

I tried understanding the reason for my existence
All I find is a puzzle with a vital piece missing
There is some promise that I would find that piece
In the light of what happens after life
Somewhere in an ethereal domain
Shaded by perception

THE LODGER

Of the many lives lived as destiny decree
I came like a lodger and I leave like a boarder
Of the many attractions and attachments I gather
I learn how patiently the creator is setting me free

LETTING GO

Affected by this and that
We grow anxious over nothing really substantial
Quieten the mind sharpen your attention
By just letting go
All things happen as they should
A tight grip holds nothing worthwhile

GLORY

In a brave effort of renewed force
We hope to reclaim glory of years gone by
Only to realize
That hand that moves the pieces
Has shifted the setting
To make way for those he kept underneath

DIVINE ARMOUR

Here today,
Gone tomorrow
Revenge and regret why harbour?
Gratitude and forgiveness you may borrow
From the divine chest of armour

SEEING

Few look to see
Others see but do not comprehend
What filters through is what is intended
A foreclosure before the fact
Of opinionated mortals
In confined boxes

POSSESSIONS

We fervently gather our possessions
While traveling on this well worn path
Only to leave without them
Yet most of life is spent
Before we realize
How fast it slipped under our feet

FEAR

Nothing gainful is born out of fear
Nothing meaningful ever came out of force
When you set aside what is expected
And all actions spring from a deeper source
You move your spirit into its freedom zone
Where everything is possible
And living is a growing experience

BRAINWASHED

Brainwashed with what's expected
We drift unexpectedly on an idle sea
Searching for what becomes hidden
After undoing the tangled messages
We set the spirit free
The sunset becomes even more magnificent
Bringing in hope pregnant with light

THE ARTIST

Children playing in the park
Fragile innocence etched
On a fresh canvas by an artist
Who grows impatient with brush and paint

IMAGINE

Living with blinkers on
Your coffers are always empty
But "imagine" the Lennon way
And fill the cup of tomorrow's wants
Just giving peace a chance

A CHILD

Drop by drop rain falls on a swollen ocean
With each child that is born
Humanity celebrates its growth
Ushering hope for its survival
This can only happen gainfully
If outdated thought forms
Do not stifle their vital contribution

HISTORY

Intrigue and mystery
Is mankind's imprint on history
Precious lessons of the souls journey
Is lost in debate and doubt
History never fails to repeat on cue
With a positive Pavlovian response

THE SEED

Roots grow deep
With branches extending outwards
The tree stands steady and well grounded
Soaking the radiance of the sun
It is the morphogenic field
Of the seed made visible
On a holographic canvas

THE PATH

Go with the flow
What have you to lose
Time finally tells
What ultimately was best
On this blinded path
From nowhere to now here

CREATION

In wave particle delight
We dance in and out
Of this perceived illusion
Created by deep pools of consciousness
Restoring balance as nature intended
Are we atomic particles miraculously put together
Chiming with the frequency of the universe
Or a divine living entity
Living in a place created just for us?

YOUTH

Youthful buoyancy of blossoming beauty
Only to fade into memorable embers
In some twilight fire of dimming light
Reminding us how fleeting time is
And how precious the moments spent can be

THE VESSEL

I wanted more
I wanted to soar
Above the mountains
Upon that note much have I been grounded
Yet this vessel keeps wanting more
To reach total completeness

HURT

Close the door
Set your feet on the ground
Hurt was never intended
The air will clear with time
Then it will dawn
There is no call for doors
And life becomes a breeze

NIRVANA

The river flows into the sea
We go with the flow
Reassuringly aware of a greater consciousness
Into which we ultimately empty
A Spirit matured with time

BLESSED

Once upon a special time
I'm told,
We get a blessed glance from above
When benevolence is bestowed
To those big and small
Of any color and kind
Some moment when
The human heart lends its beats
To the cry of a hungry child

THE SPARE

The fetters of fear fatigues the psyche
Filling the field with emotional emptiness
Driving us deeper into darkness and despair
We hold the key to let in the light
Which sets us free

LIFE

You cry in pain
And jump with joy
The highs and lows
Of an exulted life
a gift of the gods
Played out in a Maya-like dream
On an opulent stage
Blending into the sublime

THE GIFT

In years to note in some future time
This would just be a memory in the distant past
Time and space is relative to spirit
As the journey of the soul
Unravels untold karmic knots
Brought to light
In this gift of the present

SECOND COMING

They say there is a second coming
Direction is in need
The compass is lost
We are natures children
Wanting grounding

PEACE

Here today, gone tomorrow
Only darkness separates yesterday from today
Time unfurls at a precise pace
And lives are lived according to script
Setting you on a predetermined course
Question not the events that led you to where you are
It was meant to be
Nothing is out of place
Nor can you change the past
Regrets you may bear
And history is not your-story
But why bother?
It only weights you down
So lighten up
No one is perfect
Your potential is infinite and you are unique
In fact you are divine
All the world may be a stage
And life may be just a dream
But that which is experienced is overwhelming
Juxtaposed both within and without
Which makes it hard to bear

IN CONCLUSION

The drummer plays on
To the tune of the cosmic beat
Life throbs to His beating drum
And when the beat is set to change
Life takes on a new meaning
Upon a stage of changing dimensions
Where the human form adapts to an act
Not yet performed

I was born a South African. At twenty I left to India to study medicine. It was there that I was introduced to the writings of the spiritual masters of India and the Orient. I now live in Canada with my family.